# praise for ghost

As a long time admirer of John Wilkinson's poetry, ⏑ ⸻
first US book). Wilkinson's intelligence nettles, yet his compassion soothes. From in-
sidious microorganisms to macroeconomic abuses these poems offer ethical reflections
of the now and in so doing bring the "ambient usual" to heel. Wilkinson is a master of
syntax and his diction, well, yes, will drive you to the dictionary, but what better place
to be? Here we see nature unfaced by industry, yet a droplet of water works its "green
stealth." Check out "Unicorn Bait" — it's a masterpiece!

JENNIFER MOXLEY, *The Open Secret*

In writing this stunning volume, John Wilkinson begins with a phrase, ghost nets. The
phrase is not empty of real life meaning; ghost nets are, according to Wikipedia, "fish-
ing nets that have been left or lost in the ocean by fishermen. These nets, often nearly
invisible in the dim light, can be left tangled on a rocky reef or drifting in the open sea."
They are dangerous things, at least for marine life. But what they ensnare, they contain
— that can be, and perhaps always is, valuable, beautiful, and worthy of our most care-
ful attention. And so it is that the poems in *Ghost Nets* can be read as forms "in the dim
light," catching bits of language, reference, significance afloat in the abyssal culture. The
result is not so much an accumulation as a sequence of entanglements, fraught but ut-
terly exquisite, thanks to the sublime intelligence (Wilkinson's, and also poetry's) with
which the entangled elements — physical, psychological, intellectual, social, political,
atmospheric — are acknowledged. To read these works is to follow the drift, drag, and
draw of the poems — ghost nets, sad in themselves but not by virtue of what they con-
tain. That is inspiriting, inspiring.

LYN HEJINIAN, *The Unfollowing*

*Ghost Nets* gathers up a selection of some of John Wilkinson's most careful, powerful
verse. Moving from a kind of environmental or intellectual-pastoral mode, that is, close-
ly observing and valuing everything — a herbarium of ideas; hiberniculum of atten-
tions! — through poems of war, love, death, the everyday mercilessness of advanced
capitalism, Wilkinson's poetry traces personal-psychological Thought in the real-time
political and vice versa. It does so in a language that is microscopically detailed, yet
formally and musically substantial: a substance to swim in, one that has helped usher
in a contemporary Renaissance in English poetry (meanwhile, Shakespearean echoes
are just some of the ghosts caught in these nets). Simultaneously, impossibly, there's
delicacy and restraint to the "song husks" that get made this way: this is endearing
stripping. Ethereal "figments" suggest a kind of afterimage beside each word-moment,
and an "afterlife unfolds behind a hooked moon" — that stays with and changes you.
I love this poetry so much!

EMILY CRITCHLEY, *Out of Everywhere 2: Linguistically innovative poetry
by women in North America & the UK*

ghost nets

## Also by John Wilkinson

### POEMS

Proud Flesh
Flung Clear, poems in six books
Oort's Cloud, earlier poems
Effigies Against the Light
Contrivances
Lake Shore Drive
Down to Earth
Reckitt's Blue
Schedule of Unrest, selected poems

### ESSAYS

The Lyric Touch, essays on the poetry of excess

# ghost nets
## john wilkinson

OMNIDAWN PUBLISHING
OAKLAND, CALIFORNIA
2016

Cover art by Patrick Chamberlain, "now I lay me down to sleep" (2015),
Collection of Lynn Hauser and Neil Ross

Typefaces: Century Gothic, Joanna MT Std

Design & Layout by Sharon Zetter

Offset printed in the United States
by Edwards Brothers Malloy, Ann Arbor, Michigan
On 55# Enviro Natural 100% Recycled 100% PCW
Acid Free Archival Quality FSC Certified Paper

Library of Congress Cataloging-in-Publication Data

Names: Wilkinson, John Lawton, author.
 Title: Ghost nets / John Wilkinson.
 Description: Oakland, California : Omnidawn Publishing, 2016.
 Identifiers: LCCN 2016014892 | ISBN 9781632430267 (pbk. : alk. paper)
 Classification: LCC PR6073.I4183 A6 2016 | DDC 821/.914--dc23
 LC record available at http://lccn.loc.gov/2016014892

Published by Omnidawn Publishing, Oakland, California
www.omnidawn.com    (510) 237-5472    (800) 792-4957
10 9 8 7 6 5 4 3 2 1
ISBN: 978-1-63243-026-7

# contents

# Amours de Voyage

One was wax, one silk, one
metrically fluttered,
their moth-eaten slips shrunk,
wound round a rattly drum,
made sprightly round or
mount still unenclosed,
in common usage fungible:

insects corrugate my tongue,
eyes tickle, pollen, dust,
micro-organisms, leaf
hoppers compromise
the project, mess the article,
you're breaking up, honestly
I can't hear or see a thing.

Delegates may disregard
the fountain but they swig
each their own water, trudge
the slippery slope to
inspect a concrete channel
and its coping, sluggish
sinus bandaged tight in fire:

I'd been feeling wound up,
dug for gold but cut
worms aspirating earth,
sought autochthonous spirit.
Rains refresh the earth
before a cistern gulped or
ever stake was wagered,

small rain, pollen, round
on round of infiltrators
hissing steamy wastefulness,
difficult to catch right,

flux above my torpid drum.
This inky pacifical finger,
how shall it break the earth?

# Crown of Nettles

for *Maudie*

1

Rust applied to dim
the alacrity of rails, dulling
box girders, damped
down the exception

grit-bedded, fresh-painted,
casting off the sun
in a thousand spots,
each madly jiggled,

snare-that-it-is, highlight
playing whimsically
enlivened lumber,
any such exception

rusts absorbed in time:
unreality calls, hyper-
highlight cubed and floating,
dreaming its sur-

passing forest, flirted,
feinted, drew its invention
through ductwork,
trapped a glance

in a barless jail,
cutting thin canals
from their process stream.
Acid, your bright bead

carves too quickly! para-
bolic autumn

strews rays with a free
exilic abandon,

local multiplicity
makes each over, choosing
from among feeders, or
to cast its bow,

engineered from one
dangled loop, a lock-gate,
a dam. This watery
circus will figure

primarily as forest, forest
boxed for use. The false
side will bulwark
in its wet gravel,

steadfast strip the faint
cars rumble over,
heading towards the depot,
pursuing real ends.

## 2

Tamper with the skylarks'
traffic ceiling: counting
larks a pastoral
demands must wake. Frail

pagodas bob in deep space
relentlessly, re-
stocking brought them
no more mass. Lark

figments rise to implicate
scrap-memory,
their pocket temple
still high-gloss, persists

unaffected. Weather
cannot apply, these evade
the eye's catch: is
that a bird? a comet? —

an inappropriate net,
intersecting curves,
shakes out their pittering
song husks, points of

uplift, multiplied for
round reply, trill ignored
above prodigious mud.
Grub up the nettles,

ridge their stings' scatter.
While unpre-
meditated song adapts
weakly to the hydro-

carbon harvest,
and winter gets compiled,

swathes of nettles
flourish, shiver, seed,

in hotbeds wouldn't
succumb, still flowering,
why, their thronging
knots, exceeding both

decay or clean-edged mask
picked out digitally:
Such assertiveness!
Such crude strength! –

crown with their coarse
chaplet this last summer,
low mound
knotted firmly, grows.

# 3

The charge carriers
mindless of this petalled
grass, relishing
a brush with detonation,

browning off colleagues
anaphylactic through
electric stings,
sodden with antibodies,

indulged in their universe-
shuddering pokes,
excite recombinants
to their doom,

nor shall moth wings
graze inner parts,
autonomous lips' position
can't complete one kiss,

to rub and shine as it
were distractedly
ahead of the single-minded
national zoomed ray

summoning up green,
tangled with bleached roots:
kiss the only knot,
suppress the options

fluttering in the stingers
Best stay wary
of their buzzing, wet
company seeking truth:

another raffia doll or
penitent failsafe, will

coax their variable force
comprehensively out,

kind to the inevitable,
matching stroke for stroke
stump hours. Toc.
Thrives engrossingly

behind their missile shield
full of itself and what
not itself gathers
rusting at its beck,

detaining the last light
in ground cover,
kissing the dark's
rollcalling till dawn blurts.

## 4

Included with the number
whittling number,
some rough patch,
teasel of hermeneutic

decode, patch that weeps
at any contact,
breaks out in a rash
lithography, intensest

analogue, or scary probable
image coming close,
hooked to eye
in a rough fit, caught

too slowly! too retentively!
finicking one stimulus
through long-distance
hum, dismissing

won't let go but clumps
round tiny seeds,
massing the universal class
reports at terminus,

hits down at this anvil.
Early ties had shaken loose,
dodgy track adhesion,
oil-spillage, clogged

leaf-filter, what becomes
of the misdirected?
Too well-starred
their destinies collide,

snap-clean, snap-tied,
unmildewed, sharp to grab

children flexed
down their fabricator's

slippery walls, too blurred!
A halt becomes a slip and
skids to an own goal,
a cringe, a smirk

a strobe self defaced
in face of a stock image,
most likely, more than not,
eyeing the hook alongside –

Yes I'd bank on that Yes
I'd lean towards that
Yes I'd alternate
the rough with the smooth.

# 5

Accept a moon must be
roughed-up to be dragged
over the black shine:
but impulse-driven

flinging its various shoots,
umbilical but
whizzing buttoned
down, the puck scars ice,

re-inscribed as volume
slips the leash: accept
a disk of hesitancy
absconds and plashing not

lies glittering and value-free,
burrows with inertness
down ice layers,
shamed before a clip

running its heyday
polylingual like a fir cone,
shed its influences. Still,
imagine what we use

we still conduct
like water's hardware,
pulled across the murrain
with a harsh screech

shan't touch base ever
Layers though take
their time, play the lump
sum for what they can

cop, a bloody shoebox,
a refrigerated mammoth

radiate, drilling out
bee messengers

reverse-engineered
Imagine they'd fall silent,
nectar sipped by a line
run from the grave,

indexed pollen in cross-
segment cuts, sinuses
re-input, flared,
floated a dispirited tongue

to this stiff paddle by rote.
Rust and dead nettles
ramify, swing-gates
beat at the lunar curd.

# 6

Phalanstery. Ordinate soup.
Carousel. Brocade.
Welter the figures surf,
hooded and in brackets,

so that a synapse looses
undecodable bursts, trips
from this to that
hairline decision,

validating heard or budding
impulses, anxiety steers
hop-skippery, stop,
mark how a loved face

stretched across spurs
in a deep beyond –
surface re-write
sectoring a field of flares –

precedes lark integers,
appropriates a glint,
scrabbles towards
recognition, verges on near

future's touch-topography,
releases a hair-
trigger device. Soak back,
neurotransmitters:

Shush my memory. Love
cup my eye, cup my
optic, to be verified
in that cluster,

tested on each bench,
larks net the air,

the selfsame going forward
on your nod, its bright

exceptional trill
composed on a day. Steam
shifts on the chill plate,
the low-life spectre

shadows similarly as water
changes guise,
the atmospheric state in
speckle bursts hangs –

speed slows, rust commits
its antibodies.
Soil espoused. Grille
reservoir. Alacrity limbo.

# 7

Let me readjust their hang.
Let me check if an
earring's caught,
its eye-catching snag

glitters by design
through the entanglement:
and who can stick the
down-home, hooting

ambulances chase for
fresh hearts, nettle
rhizomes outdo the squalid
diagram, these radiate,

these intrude, pockmark
with their frost and green
shoots, the just-so —
see their glints throng like

misembodied insects
mash up on fixed routines,
stripping the terroir.
Weed shallows thicken

next to race and flurry,
coots rush, willows dangle,
long muscles wrench
in flaky bark. Surface

tremor, twig that drifts,
a snag, the ripple outwash
of a bag or keys lost —
all this fluke diffusion

pokes, insinuates
needles through the bank-

side receptor sites,
prods dullard beasts,

weaves together furling
selfsames and contraries.
Soft facets reassign
the digital keys,

strewn over water
chirrup, chirrup, chirrup.
Figured treble,
skylarks entertain your ear,

midges reassemble.
Did you spot their like fre-
quent the open, un-
furling, unfurling,

paling into perplexity.

## Taking Liberties

There was this tiny warp collapsed the sky,
stove the stomach in. This, not to trifle with,
brought to heel the ambient usual,
filling space where it might most matter:

      there's a blind eye between us, fluent
smut just off-centre –

Such times, with unmitigated satire,
intensified the small thing keeping step,
      a full tilt orchestra
pursued the chord inclusive, ratcheted its din
to screaming point, lugged away cloud.
A fiery babe revealed.

You'd come close. But then its stinted blazon
summons back subfusc
      In one sense glows a whitened disk.
It couldn't lodge, menially. A dropped

screw pulverised the milky filter. So I see.
Lightning will have assailed me in my cradle.

## Taking Heart

This fluke where the eye had been bountiful,
    its object crashed where X marks,
swathed in black cloth, imperturbable,
but harming tempered glass –

meteors shamefaced every head that counted,
sloppy space shrunk into an obelisk
    within whose shade
franchise had been scripted, up-to-date

free speech found its mounts necessitate
Department of State approval, global
answers fell short,
convulsed too clearly round a disk cartouche.

What dumps all over us, off what side let slip.
Such being no more than we mean,
a slice of the take
still too hot to eat. A sub, or a finger-roll,

multi-grain, served heated, napkin-swathed,
sunk as though from within by microwave,
    says yes to the offer, squirts
distilling vapour, struggles aloft.

## Meet the Folks

Mostly rubbed if not ghastly operative C
    drove a kart, stood tall,
    though borders shove
    head in a bucket:
breath of its free shaping densifies
                funds pittance furl
but saucer-like, trampled, zero character,

so cup-&-saucer-like is their pause mode,
queuing obediently
deniable orders
taken from the stars of the southern sky.
                         Sequence
human hearts pumping under smooth
frictionless, mid-tempo
head in its dunce hood,
   lacked impetus, too tractable
spread out drying silvery skins,
an installation,
punitive space of pending gave ground:

organs slopped at the base of Coatepec,
advanced systems failed.
So ask it, why should you deny yourself,
C took leave, deployed,
perusing mute tracks –
    a charge on them all
    rags on scaffold
fluttered equally warning and significant
antlers.
Democracies tuck you in and blow you out.

Then he stepped on it, he put his foot
    down, the colours mount
    throughout initialisation
    phase, quit blinking:

cloaked, by stealth, he went for it, basket
and fair face, loved with vivid graze;
                    once in place
a master take is conscientiously damaged.

# The Cages

Suspend process, no, this is the suspend process

Transparent truth, this glares too transparently

The blanket burns and exercises habeas corpus

Gelatine wafers melt, the set
eternity of hooves, trotters, pointy feet, trembles,
sticking tongue to the palate.

Hunched on the pile somewhere, hooded breath

Opaque nib, such capillary acted on what spilt

Suspend process, no, this is the suspend process

## Ministry of All the Talents

Staffed as any were noetic hull, this guy is crazy,
flailing forward through Atlantic swell.
Containers lock. Fortunately he takes on a highway,

crossing what internal devil gave him pause,
remarked I would at most. A southern coast
was a fit object, there where a finger pushes, lumps

a monumental exposure. Too loose and heavy
even so so shovel what claims call
appearance part and hope they foam in goosebumps.

## Delta Force

*after Billy Bang*

Δ

Press the objection, press the fault till
repoussé on his throat, grey in folders
it presses, it betokens too much weight
dragging shadows, one of which slumps
across the lung, like a fallback factory.
Who wouldn't enjoy a fresh strawberry
straight from the glasshouse in future?

Such was consensus in the think tanks,
seed dangling in their solution swelled.
Memos became flights of fancy, cash
poured in as virtuous practice faltered.
Serious fluid oozed from sense-organs.
A naturally present causal basis blazed.
Draw up co-ordinates, frisk the allied
megaphone for the felt-trimmed pause
and loftiness, common round these parts.

Δ

Who gainsaid,
who gainsaid the sag in any thrall,
and gave it spin, fluttering, its give gone,
the dial set to mid-gain.
Wolfowitz and Rumsfeld,
names that scrabble from the hectic
cells' churn, digested clientelism, few
were allowed to float,
the rest of them had to buckle down
a fallen world
organised for freshness.

Kind of weird.
Kind of weird the long-forgotten
sandalled up his throat,
pushing off like winged pipettes
delivering
tiny fat globules to each influenced tip.
Who could resist a whole bunch of them?
Gather honeydew,
re-run amber newsreels.
We rip what we sew,
rub our eyes till they shine anew.

Δ

He can endorse death so she'll give it
her best shot, they struggle out and make
themselves out, make out the shadows
lightweight. They were unprecedented,
walk and talk amidst the stuff of history,
swish in lightly-armoured, blurry wraps.
Rice patters on their nuptials, siphoned
off the sampan decks sanction-running,
centrifuge parts were kept by these two.
It was their new start alright, and keenly-
scrubbed shadows ran to covering flags,
killed. Money being but part of the earth,
turned over in the tilth, between claggy
waves, the mica and the mackerel, both
newly-struck and palmed until surfaced:
truth to tell it's our own image and mould.
Crude spatters too from a Gulf forecast.
Demand fruit, ripening even as handled.

Δ

Post-theory
creamy paper ashed, wrinkled
delta palm-fronds, looped lianas
stripped by fiery air. Ostentatiously
pressure is released
from pipe lines with a flammable sigh,
and candidates for posts, every exculpate
caved in, spree armies
blew mud and flesh on our account,
a casus belli, an atrocity
was stumped up:
this student in Hanoi,
does she go on true ground now,
unfretted, raked and panning
for precursors, put down your camera,
how does she connect her hasps,
her hair-grips, her little papers,
what is the weight of rice-paper?
strawberry ice?
simulcast?
thrown in her face by an American sun?

Δ

It was late at the office. The distribution
hub was loaded with dark blue or grey,
had recharged each with stereotyped,
with shopsoiled, hard-worked phrases
wrenched from their pockets, earnings
fleeced shamelessly, but each swung
along the curve of the maternal breast,
utility, light division, a benightedness
once confined to the conference room,
swiped across its guillotine of darkness.

More in low-tech style a quick boy darts
through minefields and round trip-wires,
prancing over rapids, his sample pouch
delivered to the patent office, first-use
paraphrase he snatched off a passer-by.
Whatever gets thrown at him he dodges.
Melon seeds clog the garbage grinder,
pips crunch underfoot in a loose layer,
the world on time jars then vomits out
phrased being, otherness, ipseity, blood.

Δ

Much hangs on how you approach this:
the target spools itineraries in season,
at some point every journey totals up,
so you shall be known and intercepted.
Avoid this time frame, its effective rate,
this baseline for departure, this posture
compromised by a tinder box, a prince
scarfing peanut and jello. Just grow up.
Your phrases torched villages of raffia.
Red and yellow wax scribbles hurt most.
Strawberries were in fruit, it snowed
snow most vigorously, as it was wont,
why would bad men want to split hairs,
the premises were full of themselves.
Alpines hid behind giant pin-cushions,
tryingly recursive, beyond unscathed,
a first, but I can't get out of my mind a
strawberry completely filled my mouth.

Δ

Underfoot,
underfoot was commons, rice
sacks exploded, the supply flew
following sumptuary law, how washed,
how cooked, served up, the crust
in certain cultures, the best bit, the eye
or wishbone – neither should the vessel,
earthenware or brass, be disparaged.
I am biased and I love to walk
free of shadows,
pelted with skyey floss.

In the pot,
in the pot steaming Pho, sky
jumpers kept their hands
against their sides, ready to uphold
accoutrements. These include wild tuna,
sushi grade, I stood over a rodsman,
giving him the double tap.
Our operational continuum spreads out.
Wolfowitz and Rumsfeld
heed only rice in warehouses,
the hard, all-purpose type.

Δ

The dark comprehended much too well,
light shrunken like a shiny nut, hurtled
round the mirror surface, you it winks at,
do you correct or dodge, c/f bauxite
batches under sanction, the lading note
works alchemically, lips are processing
discharge measured on the dark altar.
Tongues within holes dart and roll to shape
consignments plucked but not let fall,
afterlife unfolds behind a hooked moon

stitching light down velvet, zigzagging
tensely as a bow against a cobalt hinge,
stretching out, pulling thick, sweet blight,
compensatory shadow. Others mass
venously, pegged a forward party scrolls
through tendrils, ligaments and creepers.
Shiny orbs drag, detail gets hemmed in,
light's play slants across a shaking hole,
bellied darkness shudders and conglobes.

## The Diagram

A man in a dive aspect
A man in a crouch aspect
finger scratching right outer aspect
                          gets the gist
A man on a pedestal,
on a keystone gets folded.

A blanket of security had smothered B
in a scoop cavity, little more than a puddle
tested range to figure,
as though it couldn't feasibly render
garlands, coils, reels and space-collapsers

        groomed his capsule
        claps on his face:
        print c-range
        print k-range.
Print as he leans into the shallows.

Hollow the air with face
Dip the water with face
A man starts from scratch.

A trusted traveller floats through a quick
processing lane, eye alert
for identification, spreads, picks at
rose buds, rolls and unrolls cerebral tucks.

## Unicorn Bait

There is no I except the I I will allow.
You will not hide your face except I hide it. I
know you want to spill what you withhold.
I and you will make a team, triumphant team,
I hold your truths –

team unicorn.
Except I hide your face it will not hide.
I hold your truths, a team you want to spill,
except what you withhold, triumphant I
you made. I will allow I know there is no I

but in her lap this cornet,
this burning weapon.

There is no I except the lapping I-face.

## Not Us

Laying click by tongue will it connect
banks and briars flourish berries to hand.
A fluke, a negligent offer but horribly
pokes the skein of events that rips.

For hissing strikes this turquoise serpent
out of its brakes, pusillanimity
wields a lash on a civilised scrub,
while deep in our livers, trip-worms toil:

how old is Europe? tired with intelligent
assets, frayed in its nerves, song-
infested with whirring, drumming en-
campments, jangled life, those waiting

under the stairwell, those on the bridge,
strays and our ministers. Impulse
flays the religious, crossing their
chests, waists, we that had ousted they —

us slack-jowled and terrified, we who'd
shudder at us the prowling shadow of we,
weakening, heartening, getting a grip,
slack, though short of to blab or purify

foreign our bodies, foreign their dis-
embodiment, representative
bodies disband at a click, I, you click
not-us for their linkage, I now syllable

loose, swart, worm-riddled, berries
squish, too us, too they, but intimately
rattle and shake like a turquoise pacifier,
as spirochetes fledge mothers' milk.

## Lyric

Through dusk's blur, a flying saucer army
chopped the sky piecemeal while its schooled
accomplices, overlapped like tiles or scales,
paved the denuded face and affronted soil.

That high the swifts scooped off airy saucers,
bypassed no distant bleep. Childish pieces
knew when they were licked, once shingled
in their dappled order, jostled conformist,

like the ingredients for Peking duck, tight-
wrapped with neat submissive twirl, each
facing the face of the earth scapegraces,
faced a referral squadron, shrunk on contact.

## Laundromat

None meant to grow belligerent; the sunset
lengthening their shadows they propound
as reach, legitimate sphere. Bring in clothes,
for sensitivity add sachet after usual wash.

Millennial cults assumed the role historically;
sharp long shadows climbed as if towers –
lookouts threatened rose-tangles, trays of
drying pistachios, those calligraphic screens

threw their lacy signatures over screaming
villagers and tents. Here we go to the cleaners,
down a sidewalk suddenly ramp-like, odd
turn for slapdash asphalt, edges start rising,

then ribbon like an astrolabe, then enhance
earth knocking hollowly, supervising chaos:
upon these margins the surfeits of reason
growl out on mission, unbehested but ours.

# New Iraq, New Orleans

Once more, it strokes once more, taking away
designer clothes, the bright crop. Her swipe
was more effective than double entry columns,
humvees packed with news filters, shotgun

jolting across desert, lumbering through flood,
once more, the same strokes for different
folks naked in burkas, naked in wet hoods:
will this do, sure, this is accepted everywhere,

her swipe that charged to China, to Korea,
that takes care to the cleaners, that deferred
payments for forty years: On a burning lake,
Moloch smiles and flexes that platinum card

she authorised. Deep in the bubbling asphalt,
deep in the shit, card-switch addicts thrash
for gleams of hope foreshortened, for the here
to be now, while hungry kids gag on heritage

grits for food: corn repositions their futures,
marching in green files for Baghdad. Poised
in cute clothes that sour, that never can dry,
wheeling her idol forth from the White House,

Condoleezza chews her lip and levees collapse,
the levees she levies, the levees she levels,
and the flares go out across the Gulf of Mexico
as the flares sink back into sand beyond Basra.

# Dredge Spoils

O brother detainee. Within his middle nest
extremities, its soft regime does it not spool
surreptitious thread from a cinched
O, plucked and drawn with due diligence,

the mortal truth. No clue beyond the cell's
walls, what you wrest springs back on
glugging reels. Pipe-work festoons
round a hingeless mouth then floods

O, with what you need to know
pumped back and forth, words volunteer
their transcript, cell to cell,
        floating sticky webs play out.
How the downy nest's hissing startles,
snaps at morsels
    snaps at catechisers
caught amidst blowflies,
     O, the tainted middle
yields to the touch,
sockets that disgorge will not stop at this,
directing moral truth that floods the dying.

## Pure Cotton Buds

Over this channel, sharp pain
crosses and retreats
    opening the channel.
    And again.
So painlessly the channel silts and binds.
Pain rages back,
unbinds earth by drilling wormways,
    opening the channel.
Yes I hear you

spreading out this murk to desiccate
on hot sheets.
Mud-flats would be thin but apt to clarify,
mud-flats would bind like silicate,
    glistering,
pathways are exposed across the trellis,
earth's blade-shuttled breast
                yields
what might soothe, if pilotless –
I know your voice.
    I see the condensation.
It was thought to have been condensed.
Stretching, it feels, could be my specific.
    Anchor off. Reverse in.

## Lane Etiquette

What means let condensation clear?
Through the rear view mirror's cut
of precious cheek, inchoate wheels
pass comprehending, so the reliable
truck tarps my green fear and letters it;
misted glass, wiped to read intention,
clears a concreted constricted throat.

At night flesh draws shade around,
pent like emotional versions super-
imposed on neck or foot: red impress
squirms while it rides on my heart's
musculature, the shade responsible
for that flitch was sealed and bottled,
a red stamp overprinted its window,

confirms all functions outputting OK.
A checkered past now thrusts ahead,
wipers snatch the toughened glass,
rear view compensates for narrow
tunnel vision, breath fogged up signs.
Hotshots drive bereft of life qualms.
Reliquaries display the living senses.

## Neda Agha-Soltan, Travel Agent

Fold the sky, insert into its envelope
slicing the tongue. What got into you, figurant till
suddenly jog controls, prise a clamped door
along the ridge in mid-air. Splintered
not on cue sucks door rages, drags, crawls.

Sky folds religiously they'd ditched.
Rivet slots i.e., as per. Return to blanks
militias, calmed by dead shows and dreamt repeats.
Painted arc rats skittering from flour.

Whiffs of cloud string out, then solder
lines out to rights. Neda, one more name,
a walk-on part. What got into you, flamed
imperial measures, godly screed from blue to black,
Kufic, fold sky and solder in its ridges.

## Victoria Soto, Teacher

Across dreaming continents
a child's hand grips a child's shoulder,
            a child's stamped eyes
stumble, and the broken
children recombine in dreadful houses,
            scrabbling at the stuck
doors, at the unfindable exits
in houses grown-ups grow to diminish
            although trapped in them,
cave or corridor or loft or dormitory,
the shelved room with its cooling kiln.
            Children still assemble
from sound and sight particles that drift
amid grown-ups in open beds,
as if their dreamt crush could reprieve
            file on file of locked steps.

# Formation

Who was warm stone,
smelt of flint,
felt like moss and lichen, my
reflected mother.

Then falling at an angle
chill rain promulgated,
I claimed basalt for my so
cheerful pillow,

pillow rock or mortar,
neck brace
or executioner's block.
All turns about –

through the night I
dissolve in hot pumice,
breathe basalt,
cooling my made mother.

# Terre Haute

The bell of glory hung on its own recognisance above,
Wan moony fish. A meadow spread for fiery spew
Got similar. Well-fed the squabbling truth addicts
Streamed away, I felt wrung-out and stunned, much as

Avidly we'd sought it, all befell. Just one tick before,
I'd strapped myself to justice at my re-evaluated post.
Glide path had shone in bleeps. Always the revealed
Flap away, but truth had little need for the thin casts

Streaming in their love of violence, furled in their lean-
Burn aspiration. So I never. So some other party
Flourished in assembly language, so the fruit they urge
Clumped round the bomb bays and military laurels.

That would be the best I could expect. Look up a side-
Effect and any agent links to any fierce disturbance,
One being sudden death. The entire dusty web starches
Like a uniform, not for nothing that result grudgingly

Strung across the lake jobless heavers at holes. Frozen
Shanties drop cluster lines and fish hang like puppets,
Confident their buoyancy might ride winter out: I
Thought of their ballooning transport, of deep drafts

Lurching through canals that stitch once-cloven seas,
Crossing air control sectors. As crows beset Terre Haute
Patrolling the ice, gasping shoals break through cloud
Blackened in their Death Rows, flocks petition idols

For the pittance reeling out, upbeat in mercilessness.

## Timing Chain

Back lane had been furnished, was upholstered, cause
Wouldn't aspirate but turns on its wheel a fleabite spark,
Spark that hollows in its mineral wool by smoulder
This cave and the next one drawn up and immobile,

Habitually to keep a vestal smoke-adept, performance-
Ready one with force majeur then broke the line,
Torque which settled on the mind as though pitched
Let slip a ratchet then more is sectioning what grieves;

So each chapelled in its wool or tallow, hunkered down,
Took the full force, the stanchion wouldn't buckle
No matter what hit. Food sprang out of roadside bins
Even while mechanics wrenched away and fretting

Pooled at coughing cylinders failing by some margin,
Stayed within their vapour pits undeterred by tremors.
Going the full length would shrink from disclosure.
They cap the finials well short of what's asked for.

Rev up to beat the first lap with accompanying notes,
Imperative straight if a grand sweep that was. Tam Lin
Coughs at full-out choke, paling to the $n^{th}$ degree,
Such faces have to breach the next outer face of face

Subtracted either way, as though a fuse trail could jump
Between pockets. Stash the furniture between stars
So each star gets forced down in its cubicle, years
Compact like telescopic pointers of light, pinpricks

Stretched along warped time. You put a human face
On a forecast, make the best of the early fireball crash,
But Tam Lin you smoulder low in a cloacal galaxy,
One lump among myriads ensconced there now naked.

# Rainclouds

Steel-plated, copper-bottomed but reflecting low
Activity, heaves a gouting cloud for this bestowal –
And in its thickening, in its involutions growls
Then pads, all too real and physical. No contact,

No direct channel, even if lightning crazing jelly
Air fills the vacancy. On earth nothing weighs,
Most like this dope fridge, what can it symbolise?
Nevertheless high airiness bestows a needed mass,

Mass bestowing weight on the dry cracked cloth,
Chalk falls and is frittering, dust jettisons in white
Seed explosions against walls, the jellied light
Blinks in time with clouds' complicating. At best

A surveyor narrowing her eyes on a mobile screen
Chock with scurrying inaction, focuses as though
Given due weight, and such goes for all those
Who sleep in dust but definitely leave their mark.

Once more to rush at floating booms, once more
To clear the harbour. It's a bonus for posterity
The dead should make their bed in preCambrian
Schist, that surely every last drop can be expressed

From the rustling of their sorely flattened dialects
Making haze churn. So here goes. Standards drop,
A golem shapes dust and vapour, parturient,
To lower on its haunches serving all generations:

It's visible. This does not finish with the signature
Fantastically elaborated. What went out as a rough,
Fills empty matter between sky and inmost fire
With shocks of forces quivering still in realisation.

## The Master of the Well of Life

Turn the golden spigots, *tu supplex ora, tu protege,*
*Tuque labora.* Though night letters vow retribution,
Queues of local people clutch their suppliant bowls
For soccer balls, cigarettes, T-shirts soaked in blood.

Thieving masts pull down high-grade data packets,
Angels peck out eyes from operatives, cawing loudly.
The carnal sheath of suffering gets screwed tighter.
All the world's wealth flows into the bloody spurts –

Hills that fumes imbue, seas floating oil immantles,
Forts, embassies and black stick forests, manumitted
Into tribute, croziers and plungers and pikes bristle,
Converging where a hunk of meat expressing SIGINT

From which those three estates drink the requisite
Encouragement, the credulous, the credit officers,
The office of the credo, that with dripping mouths
Wet this piece offered also: What of it? What of it?

# Olympia

Offered on a plate the all
              drawn into herself a gateway
stitched-up
interstices
without a retort bulge,
              so all one is offering its loose-
limbed collocation yet.

.

Yes yes forced to want.
Yes wanting with pent fury.
              The blue-purple bloody trunk
clunked from its dispenser
sealed in thick clear plastic to Receptor
              throwing up aghast A.
Thus were the long and short ever
summarily twisted.

.

              Gag on it and blindfold.
Crush before a line of goblets tossed one.
Made each setback harness.
Bush that in spring vomits bees and
in flowering, ammonia,
scents jolts of wind never will disperse.
              Flying range, pierce
multitudinously.

.

Stood amok.

         Loosed paths.

           Split pods crackle.

Seed forces through infected stitches.

Can this love be restored?

        It ails, not outgoing.

        Cut back to festoon


Jacinthine coronal.

.

## Set Down

Mild as the indescribable beckons, and optional,
reaching with replaced limbs, proffering a new cup
brimming squalls and joy, the in-dweller swops
parts ceaselessly so a florid gaze submits and turns
composed towards its steady exhibition to itself.

Gently set aside the knife at the belt, a dusty cheek
propped on a stand in plaster recognition, pleases
the in-dweller plucking it to join an assortment
gazed on by a self-approving gaze, to be applied
to a half-mask anxious its match should not falter,

not again. Clear-cut the hidden shines, for shame
casts brilliant copies, scrutinising them for faults
permitting truth to leak through. Each disabused
by the gaze it is its work to hold steady, evidently
mounts a replacement cheek while seemingly fixed.

## The Summons

The harbingers are come.
They web earth with their antennae
in gold, they pester
fluttering and fluent children,

mortals sought them out, a cathode
charge on the once dead.
Are we agreed? Does
attraction churn the earth with tongue-

twisting cast, whether
paddle or propellor or two soles:
are we agreed this is a mast
and not a spar bleaching –

how if the spar calls back the buzzing
voluble transmissions,
and positively
grounds our would-be forerunners.

## Shop Floor

I suffer latencies.
I look myself in the eye waiting on
my brutal glint,
but.

What teeth are these?
A claw hammer floats past reach.
Its stock shadow laughs
at a delay

beneath any notice,
in drafting stage my model slumps
on quiet salt –
lost science lies.

I watch the sun
dock against a terminal,
steel lagoon
shifting to fragment faltering rays.

## In Suffrance

Tree-lyres raise their tails
behind the brilliant pasture.

Condensed matter
visibly expands. The wood

that was stopped, sings.
A bunch extends permission.

Open the shores, the banks.
Open the obdurate. Light

outdoes its lighting,
laid on the still concealed,

defying we creatures
lit to shed our armature.

Soughing laps the tight trees.
Whence does. Whence.

# A Claim to Land By the River
for Christine Adams, because of Adrian Adams

The sea exacts the least light, and the least light scrims
over sand, plain clothes.
A moving article, my car say, ploughs ahead yet paler,
specifies clean past:
its precedent would have been fulfilled were the ocean
a knickknack vault, a locker,
     or were asphalt
decked with clues – the clue
points to settled worth, its light-sealed idiom
         But no way –
air stirs, the disappointed lees
shift and mutter failing to consolidate, fritter outward,
lost to limpidity;

a brilliant scrivening that floats above the sand's shift/
well possibly,
for by such lights nothing changes, one fevered rush
rips and crumples and chucks rags
against a backcloth which had played neutral, drips
white spirit in dissolving stains. Maybe
once,
but light still unshuttered, light without shadow blades
     signs off on the crust
it holds hostage. Only sleep ranges,
vague tittle tattle licks into shape and what makes shift
ground dazzled under lien,
orchestrates this work for many hands, this story,
     just how maize is planted,
goats milked, chickens fed,
how father's time
turned soil while cancer worked along his spinal wick,
no it's impossible, a seed patent
spoken for and measured,
     turned soil distractedly;

story-tells below what sugars over, below its slathered
vouched integrity
        revealed truth
rational faith/
community of praise/
        applies a corporate thin film
mindful of their assets, filmed, filmed then cropped,
disinter their dead in coffre nakedness, slightly glazed
still march according to their register,
turning in their graves,
        shuck-headed, fully-armed,
maintained a strict order underneath combed wavelets,
then, then, for future reference
necessarily get
dragged beneath blood-stiff scrim trouncing resistance,
rank on rank consigns their scant plunder –
        These indentured

mash up where the flower regiments this time of year
expresses now, rotating bulbs
with dead tubers,
sheet of colourways laid out on sand for summer's
late sunburst effect, reconciled in storehouses,
treasure buried, massacre forgotten, mash up sweet
profit for the big man,
        natheless
        natheless
the speeding bullet counts out and the car
struggles in red mud the wheels churned up glutinous,

peasants shake the corm boxes wireworms still infest,
breasted black suits, white shirts meaning trouble,
        missionaries re-stir
a shifting plot, an ant-mound, derisory but feathered
sub-plot, like a frigate bird that wheels
imperturbable in tempest, troubling through calm,
not surveys merely but rotates the earth like a paddle/
round the frigate bird the unendurable heat is stirred/
        fan blades chop against a film winder,

heat-imaged
offices and voices hive, rattling pots and pans
in their braille galley/ What I want: Roots Train,
Super Étoile:
What I want/ No Thing-Malarkey/

picked open this container-load
spilt then spurted out the transubstantial vein of milk,
the tumultuous honey,
smitten rock, a cleft that spat out tree-picks for forests,
        fish flop round the stockade –
for only the impossible makes possible,
only the precluded
        swings the gate, and there the rut of land fruits,
impossible in truth. *Kounghani*.

# The Whole Deal

Normally 'whole' meant its shaken box,
auto-timer or dissolving glaze
   smoothed breaks and lesions,
but this 'whole' made legacy
stockade a highway bypasses – did
one say 'cocoon' or 'coupon'
   clipped within set time,
just lay its contents out unvarnished –
Start again, they regroup,
   open mouth
the pollinating moth rummaged freely,
spoke of Indian Village,
spoke of Gold Coast,
   sniffing at its lines
like they were pay-offs, you were so
ashamed to let float:
breath-laden were the pods that wallow
drowned in sleet and cuckoo-foam.
   Still, you stick it out uncovered,
what else.

Look lively plaintiff but show caution,
   watch your mouth.
Speech may fail,
but spoken-for now copies curves,
   matter of fact
office malls and the mosquito signature
inanely dim. Ductwork
overwhelms the evening's pretty face,
   all its circle
moth-nibbled, thrown into array,
scrawls in plaster
   names unreadable, distorted,
laths and tarpaper crackle in late heat.
A ball attributes sentience to prairie,
and the eye

identifies, believing it entire,
    but the eye is obstructed
by that capsule,
liquid slurps down its nonstick surface,
flares fringe Hammond, Gary Indiana:
Minus these its stops and tracks ·
    no ball, no dice, no play.
    Nothing follows.

Step on the gas, floor it.
· Tramp the relic, tramp the jagged femur.
The whole will raise them retrospectively,
aura raise the bunch
uncreased like manga boy-girls,
their blemishes dabbed off with spirit,
dry bones walk:
    such phantoms harry
sad-sacks, heavy-laden, but seem more
forgivable because perfect,
flutter without fingerhold or handle,
    shiny, not one care,
pass through pools of balked emotion
unaffected, ·
slosh about in their own sense of injury,
· they are immune, their capsules
never split or melt:
    pain even to its bearers feels other,
nor fear nor pleasure
makes impress,
the great hoardings
    blank themselves,
favourite radio lapses,
    electronic tumbleweed
beckons in full beam, and occupants
of any driving seat must set their cap
by global positioning,
    even over a precipice.
· Not to make a thing of it.

The thing came to its head all the same,
the thing burst.
Hunched convulsed beside the toll-road,
skimmed and grazed, who couldn't
    see it for what it was.
Pre-emptive stop-over,
no dispute.
The righteous have to weigh each soul,
    others' flesh
transported through glass airlines
was just gagging to be weighed,
gagging to recapitulate,
    the thing came to its head:
the thing was discontinuous yet history:
the thing was smithereens yet whole:
across the booking hall
excited baby heads bob,
    mirroring the shininess
of reconstructed cheeks, flesh
smoothed by being burned: This
patina fulfils their need,
the wretched fontanels exploding
    make them whole,
who shrink from touch, whose dry lips
glaze over,
    glass will cure their malady,
it was enough to have once kissed
    open-mouthed,
the thing reached that specific point,
that's the thing, or was,
where shrapnel glossed, light played.

In shattered glass they see themselves
    perfected,
sun no longer drags
    across their bodies,
lurching forth to desiccate and trouble:
sight of daily drag, subtracting years,
their unspoiled lids shrug off,

nor corruption scarfs the bud –
transports beckon, glassy transports
glitter in their eyes'
detached lenses, twists of paper, verses
muttered like conclusions:
 The thing came to its head:
 the thing then says:
it was enough to have once sipped at
emptiness, to kiss the air,
to pocket it:
images decay, the body will decay, let
all be shone up and effaced
in heaven's protocol, in vacant glamour
let the whirl of glass and bits of flesh
be sorted, wheat from chaff, sheep from
goats, obsidian from clear and present,
paradisiac elements from the fat
belly, rubbish complexion, eczema,
 succubi consulting sleep.

The thing is some get sorted,
shine up like neonates make light
about the watching area,
take their lustre from the travellers'
decay.
 I call halt in disbelief.
 I fill up. I ask more.
I love throughout the orifices,
 hugging the corruption
of flesh, mind and heart,
smashed windows, burnt demesnes,
 heaped tires
chemical fog day is breaking through.
Laburnum pods crackle.
 Soft
lenses shower to earth on time to
set impressions.
  The subject
broached once more, gets riled up,

light throws its inevitable pall
       upon the miscellanies,
survivors queue at the dressing station,
blink as though conceivably whole,
behind their crusted faces
       pass conceiving.

## Ode: The Light Thickens

The light thickens. Down the hallways, in the harbours,
round parking bays, revelation plays its known tune,
  in the flesh a glass funnel turns,
flesh rigid as a sumptuary who keeps watch
inwards. Past these walls, flesh creeps and stuffs
the biosphere. Enjoy living forms available to take home.

How many anuses are gagging daily in glass towers
on repeat, how many doll faces lathering with sperm?
  People in glass houses
fold themselves in glowing flesh as their own
filaments, they re-purpose every frocked
bough as if it could be spread or conveniently wrapped.

Diagnosis lays out the unarguable. Diagnosis buffs up
dumped flesh, the forest also marches like an overture,
the art object sucks value.
  Five have entubed
the polonaise rack, scoped heat waves in peristalsis,
slapped through glossy pages where ephemera get staged

behind the troweling light, dangling their entrails like
tentacles of mid-century jellyfish. Clamshell
insulators gape hungrily in nacreous pink foam moulding.
  These belong to systems other
than the stack of flesh blinking alongside,
even if seed mussel vents do cluster at its cinderous dome.

Well time to kick back and ogle. Time to lay out eyes
for an apocalypse, tangles ventilate a cylinder
beneath foaming clear gloop poured in at one end.
  Reaction intense,
but why does nothing clench like a core
within an aureole of missed shots as flustered, disheveled,

hauling while stretching one foot off the ground,
you lunge for an access key, scrabble through a sand-map
of dreams, typeset and bound in Vietnam? Blood
in ejaculate, or a virulent strop ejaculation
streaks dawn. Assessing what panned out,
     to block or throttle might have capped

a flank vent, seen the grey volcanic glass balls deflagrate,
a boiling retort uphold its toffee
outline through a triple pass under Ishtar gate,
admission still denied to those too obviously pleading –
     some kind of neon tube
processes data, bubble tea, swollen globules of tapioca

blurt glowing rows and eructate through flesh in plumes
like maleficious stars yet unformed.
So œdema traps the transfusion. What wells and pulses
across veins and maps of frost, what drabbles skin,
     what interior expressed,
trickles its due measure, each in supping at his spigot

feels a roused ball discharge inside his cheek
a taste sensation, a noise sensation, an eruptive sensation,
these drain onto the vocal cords, causing choking.
The light thickens. Trees volubly silt with trees,
trees wave like infolding trees, a falling
tree lowers slowly through the light ingesting its sap.

# Ode at the Gate of the Gathering

Reflexively I cracked my knuckles.
What Cook said through his hands stops the breath
flowing from its bunker,
leaked across grilles, to curl in on itself:
Do you comprehend one thing?
    What had knocked and pounded
fell apart in sections then fled
      Took its pulse
and up with its folly trembled,
        hollow cry
departing from the drifter laid upon his concrete,
stripped of his cry, a line of air:
the thing is
that's all you ever were, it shot back
beneath the vaulting, the unrising ribs.
Snow convulsed, it was the streets' collateral loss.
New formations were that brutal.
    Follow where a breath insists,
sped through pendant gates. What Cook says goes,
his suitcase clasps the silences,
their suitcases are packed and now dawn filths.
    Hang on, hang on just one minute.
I left behind my necessary.
    Chop chop. Speed up.
      Lip the drape.


We are anomalous and childed as such,
this crying hollow has exposed each scaly novelty,
    air-licked, antennae flopping
streamlined through a reconditioning chamber,
pink phosphorescent wands laid flat,
squeezed as
    from an icing bag, hoar-frost-bright,
a voice without marrow shouts "I shall
be staggered with my first blush"

or "this bloody thistledown,
blown off my project,
    horsehair dispersed": this one example
creasing up with shame,
blew about the area like a franked permit
let fly into flakes.
Its cancellations show who loitered breathless...
and repented thoroughly.
                An arterial
balloon blows its stopper, many stoppers
        clustering like fish eggs –
    Hang on –
was I Child number eight or Obstruction 3 million
rising, like as not? Rising as the snow
dragged its cloud?
    Gird impoverished. The singspiel
of split children thicker than the cantilevered ivory
(commercial) envelopes my hollow voice.

Under guidance child kit
    greys like a pupa
Children hang in rows,
    glister fades –
grey like a moonstruck
    house of pupae
    house of cambric
tosses back
headscarf after headscarf,
thready voice
loomed, cowled in grey.
Lines comb the foreshore,
    horses in mid-stride
limbered up,
faltered.
    Tufted children,
hooked among
    grey filaments,
smoking wicker,
Simi bugs,

the thing is
electricity can offer
maturation like silk.
    Hang on,
robed in lost wax. Hang on,
incandescent marrow.


Cook struts into a snowstorm he winches back,
takes aim, as take were to receive
    and this were the only action possible
under the level eyes of Cook.
Stone is what I does my business with quoth Cook,
I'll get my mitts on it, I'll get the job finished.
He's in a strop, he's foaming.
Thou hast brought me forth.
    The splash of a rhesus monkey
      steams. Callipered
and compassed.
          Light snatches cowls of sleep,
swipes them from the tufted and new-whelped, they
have no appurtenances to speak of,
    hangs them out, pegging them
to dry like advent dials. Except one I poke at,
testing my scimitar.
    Chop chop chop.
The splash his victim makes
reddening a burnt crust of snow is creeping on stone
paving in the undervault.


    Concentrated phonic pith.
Grit rasping a patrol skirting shit facilities,
caked mud burnside.
    Lighting grates.
Put forth his hand and touched my mouth.
A transom rattled up against the street-level brow,
blanked the screen a drifter
    crouched behind.
That's an egret. That's a black crane buffetted.
Fluffy things get chopped, they naught defray,

figuring in poke stars,
a billion mayfly nymphs rush to fill
    a backpack. Portmanteau. Organiser
crammed with butchered limbs and pouched organs.
Right you are.
Cook says here you have a crack. O right,
rub the stone.
His fist pumps methodically but bruising
won't pitch up nor potash purple spread its stain,
although the pit is painful, pit shrivels
in on itself,
left-over bones seethe in a mean gruel and scraped
gloved shuffle keeps the fist pumping,
visits have been cancelled and that's all there is
    shoved in a cash mouth
below a speaking grille,
    look, he thinks
    the sun shines out of his mouth.
Cook trounces the black dough and at first a foggiest
and then a glimmer then the silicate in tilth
then the dawn bruise then fret blazes,
down the lip splashes amidst slush
in glowing boulders and in fist geodes that the grey
children stumble over, dead to all appearances
    wait upon air.

Chop chop chop
    No pause before Cook's fingering
dissevers.
End exchange.
    Where's the bruiser, where's Cook?
Where's that roughhouse bastard
prettifies the buffed-up,
rasps the shining peel to
warm up a bit, impinge,
    does the necessary
right here and now,
    like thumps him with his club glove,
duffs him up a bit,

then a lesion vomits out silverfish,
dawn smears over scales,
     *ink reddening the stone*, actual
bloody earful, tap
the earful this swills, drain out the susurrus:
which on quiet waters murmurs like a buzzing fleece
Cook thinks he sees right inside of, *positive*
a buzzing fleece that drapes blinking towers,
     towers plot position,
watch your mouth, just watch your mouth
and stub your long-tended shout:
breaks are garrisoned with status displays,
     fleshly tables,
          clay that weeps figures.
Poor dumb mouths, you let in nothing do you,
               suppling the lip.


               Sometimes invincible a grey
base station floats forward disavowed, every
lattice window splays out some whip-smart quiver
like a tubeworm,
     split pink antennae,
crisply those were fiddleheads over which fresh
form and curd sensation emanate
to crawl across the sky's depth like central-
heartened yak herds blindly glutting on their pass:
Cook scoops them up,
these'll come in handy,
garlanded with maggots and fly-crowned.
     Browned-off birds walk into nets
acquiescently,
     fruit shrugs its peel,
and high ogives shake in vapour trails, vapour trails
stiffen as bamboo submits to hoop in steaming gently/
Nabatean gate for leopards, vaults
clouds infiltrate, switchback to stampede
Mongolian horses, horses give birth to
     /more void
     You are unfathomable/

more void/
Slice-and-dice shades into much worse.
New seasons hit the racks. Beware the fluent tiger.
Cook staggers to a fire door
and sticks his head out, brandishing a cleaver,
                                        deerskin sweeps behind
his juggernaut, a lotus root he has his eye on
gilds itself, chryselephantine: vanishes in gleams.
    A few remaining hands bunch
rheumatoid, asphalt rucks the runway,
evacuated children sleep out, their suitcases
disgorging their effects,
    air seeps through wattles
    sucked in
by embodiments
    thrown together any-which-way,
put to useful toil, bent over iron pots,
curved in on themselves so forming solid hands.
    Soon they're sent on detail,
tell you what...
Cook he gets urges, he has issues, he desquames
        chop chop chop
opposing thumb.


If they grow in filth
they emerge as Filthflowers,
if Filthflowers do endure
good turn they scuttle
Prime Dawn.
The cuts of Prime Dawn
breed maggots,
and their extract
curdles into Fiddleheads.
Fiddleheads uncurl
and slide like Silverfish
gleaming as they
bloody straighten out,
much like Tibetan
script or nymphs in molt.

After a thousand days
nymphs fly south,
they are subsumptive,
but they flutter out
like insects in general,
they are optioned by
Potash Industries.
Investors cash out,
converting potash into
Dry Leftover Bones.
The spit
of Leftover Bones
leaps forth as deer,
the broth they make
feeds communities. Men
imagine Simi bugs;
Simi are the bugs
Cook favours,
clustered about the stalks
of Filthflowers,
one good turn
flipped on the griddle
Got me like I'm toast.

     Shut that cakehole, shut it.
Cook's grumbling deep in his cups like bereft:
   So these uprisings of fish
shoal in ripples for display, bees compile
beneficent plunder as was both decreed and meant:
Thou art a swift dromedary,
a den of dragons,
   how shall I put one over,
how shall I put one across,
    tally herds across my clicking fingers,
      through my clock eye, force
catalogued and branded beasts
down an impasse of butchers and fishmongers,
spring the latch seized at the gate of the gathering?
     Thought-meat and mind-beetles

jump form, hit the deck. Swap gaudy ribbons
childed in the 3rd moult.
        Be not afraid of her several faces
Chop chop chop
   – faces will be snatched
off in the back cut, the blind alley,
   – faces will en-
gird each fiddlehead now curling
from the filthflower in its vacant and wrenched turn,
    imprint the panelled stacks
of air piled upward
    to face one snarling face, reverberatory,
       stripped jaw ablaze.

The thing is the thing is…
     No debate, sunshine, no contest,
no two ways.
    I feel I'm drifting off.    Drop to lap.

# Courses Matter-Woven

for J.H. Prynne
*furthering many*

*Unhaunted quite of all but — nothingness?*

1

Pressing Emptiness can't adapt to scurryings not audible:
    stopped down mutely to the clay, stern
Vision buoys up still, through cushions
and through influx, a windsock prolapsed in bronze.
    Peewit calls a dipping, dotted course.
      Shining binds the Instrument, analysis
is on a hiding, don't start to think otherwise,
cardboard and tape measures brought for a maquette —

nonetheless a shuffle-deck of feelings slips from cartoon
parameters, each from each, quietly,
      persons run ragged for a stroke
careens just then and there as though it swung against
face-forward, swelling it with what boded ill
beneath the flyover, in the stall underneath straw:
    emaciated palm tree ribs, jutting hips,
 simultaneously these expand and organs hang from them,

human brain even, what activity
can be detected in these? Values *en cocotte*? Whispers
also that everyone agrees they ride on the ability to ruffle
edges whether stuck down or gently nodding.
    Ruffled blue tissue awaits its fruit,
ruffled petals spill their scent, awaiting moths' signature
      Until light interrupts,
lathe-cuts a pattern with its shine and slick, figures out

Vestigial Inwardness, till a notched tape pinches a balloon
to get its reading: that inflicts welts:
    invisible respondents pluck and prod,
harrying a Vision of Humanity,

drawing blood that stains oilily the lacquer dogs slither
over, dogs abound and won't be whipped in, –
        rotates in its collar Liberty, sweet Liberty.
At this the seas roar and the votive gulls hung by threads

pitch sickeningly, even as the broken pack
is drawn off by a smell of meat, mills about within its new
restored form.
        In the collar, in the gimbal
spins the human chassis, limbs outstretched and
excruciated in the warp ends of longitude and latitude
picked off from her fingertips, casting
bird coverlets and aeroplanes on predatory mission,

rigged for their remote destinations, brought about.
But she now shrinks within our sights.
But she forms the upside or the downside.
        Birds line up again to test the waters,
sipping at foam.
So she is assembled by numbers.
She kneels in her bracket further bracketed in echoes.
Scurryings and scratches fade, even when the crick throat

gripped in callipers, gasps
across its casing a dashed-off profile moiety while her flip
        upholds a scentless spray of cowslips:
either/or
compounds the Real but what does her cheek press?
        Sung performances fail to
disarray the orange suit or disintegrate the kevlar
before the invisible audience dropping in on this tableau.

## 2

Smuts are they or moths flagging over bright instruments,
    flopped about blood and piss threads,
late drunken shouts empanel Emptiness's swell.
Close to Form moths hesitate, holding pattern
      proof against a train's shout,
      squeak of a stile. Colourfully interspersed,
      accepting white and fawn Spontaneities,
bloom not made for store brings them out of themselves,

responding where each wing-set of dust whose hieroglyph
aggressively putting forth
      clash of clash of clash
         You want it
      clash of clash of clash/ beyond the gate, the monitor –
Who am I a gatekeeper running backwards through gates
and slamming them into your face,
    slap slap applicator/
         This Here, which hereinafter

wrenches stamens loose from the orbits of Encompassing,
      point by point in Agreement,
    disfiguring stops and pinning charts
until they match, she carved thee for her seal
functions restore and dibble
earth beneath its frost brocade: their traces of Thought
stir in real-time display, their flutter
musses leaves endearingly while stripping off chronic bark:

What batters at the door
    What compounds the offence
    Nothing presses with
    inverted polarity. Nothing there
breaks my neck,

exposing a balloon, a squelched condom,
                vivid view/undo/back of the head:
Hover-flies zoom in on flowers they select as moths feast

low in theirs, along with Timings similarly. Each at its
   wildflower, trackside escapee
or self-copulating cultivar, riffles through a seedbox
  blackened like a casket,
swathed in bloom; a rose imbued despondent on a lattice

cups what flies its way, the eye in it hooks light and is torn.
Liberty slashed like a vernal or shocked heath.
  Leave edges unfinished. Impossible to bring flush,
squeezed back in two minds but close.
    Office hours screw-cap, per-
frict business practices and deep-died:
pollen filtering regardless of season or of source –
Cutting edge immobiliser licks out the only one I cherish.

  How can nothing
  in itself be cancelled?
  Hold and lock
  gains a firmer grip on emptiness.
Emptiness condenses in her presence gulping its presence.

# 3

Push Here: pink rose reset reset.
Too much give saturates the button over-eager to engage.
    Heather millions think wafting warm air
unbounded while its filmy bag breachless,
will pay court to a garden true to their Cast of Mind
as though lobbed into mind its fruits will evermore befall:
There is no place like no-place blanks,
        before this null the tulle folds in on itself,

when Nullity is tremblingly transpired, a contingency felt,
uproar shakes them from the stalks. Stay
your Axiom as was a singular world pupped.
    If so Thought
      would not turn. Seldom pocket moth
broke the sun's stride. Does the sun count its paces?
This or that balk
brings about detours of blood and bone, takes the form

of space for a moth or an invented right-angle joint
self-presenting in its snug container or in memory foam,
cut into privet.
      So Emptiness is shaped: how empty can be the sky
fine fuel droplets, drones beyond description,
falling and reflected light, the mirages
cut from prescribed cloth and lain
obsequiously into the western niches, keep in movement?
           breaks my neck.

Fast as thou wane she stomps numbers stacked against her
as and must I gatekeeper turn against statistics:
      How can columned light enfold.
      Pressure
points nail a slew map reference, crook of elbow to one
    hanging foot arch. De-
cadencing from where it would surpass. Tight bend,
outline and cold creeps, plantation trapezoids
whose squadrons rotor out to prospect, their shingle

Thought accounts for the earth: windows supply
liquidity, global
view is tendered to its intussusception,
offering its flank as to stroke of blood count. Bounty
is suspended temporarily. Strike then the knell
     cramp crooks together, hovering in limbed Apotheosis,
O cobalt coast, O fleet I, O new arrival

period long decayed, unmoors violet tacks
articulated so securing promise ever sweetens the barrens –
     welcome! 140 space underground copy die!
The converse was not mass but dispersal.
Opposites distract. But every noble insect that visits,
foreboding the Idea of such Uplift
        tethered like a dirigible on the skyline, ceramic
blue before the sunfall turns it cupronickel

tugs at the heartstrings, dangerously.
As a result the canopy simply turns inside-out and the silk
ribbing collapses and its tongues bunch marigold.
     The sun stays,
its vapours folding in, foregoing and succeeding sucked.

# 4

Once you get down to it you got to get up.
Though wind rattles ill-fitting windows in the
warehouses, it even so must consolidate
you well-wrapped with gales on that headland
named Previous. While there's scant gap
between markers and a melody petering out,
that doesn't mean the foot slips the stirrup

nor that the pieces won't fit back in their tin.
In fact they do but then won't stop swelling.
Growth was what we had expected, so
not much to complain of there. Poor yearlings
piled on the pounds and even the elderly
wouldn't shrink obligingly but overflowed
their chair seats. Unions leagued and clubs

amalgamated. Eyes bulged. A bit unsteadily
I pulled myself together well into place.
If you want to stay in one piece then get down.
No shelter for the locals or a traveller either,
lizard tongues, enormous hands, breasts
that topple the mother and crush her brat.
We might become unmanageably extended.

The Grouping hereinafter hunched in a ditch
alongside. Not to say hands wiping air
crumpled like a vast sky staked by the flaps,
corresponding Parts fused, it was only
once this Unity broke they could assemble
red-eyed, arthritic, squatting in their own shit,
fiddling with buttons, numbers and timers.

Here Splintering ends. Contained explosions
clear the air, and Rage creates a replicable
device, primed for a passer-by. Would it be
ill-advised to consort with them, inner
floaters that expressed might clump causing

who know what Interactions? He wipes hands
on a grass verge: Notice: he walks over it.

# 5

No leachate can persist in solution. It might crystallise.
Fall into line would be more it. Canada Geese
used to fly in V shapes but directories
darken skies: to one attach the term 'Exemplary'.
      But amongst all individuals
more flocks flock and throngs throng,
and this biomass choking the outstretched neck
is meanwhile rippled by the glittering chaff that interferes.

      A great shit storm hit.
      Exorbitant tranche.
      Aspirators panted.
      Wrathful chromosome.

It never skips a beat, the sky erupts, dawn chorus scatters
blissful Versions,
      arcade machines, utilities spit bleeps and pings,
flash up fault codes in block numerals.
      Heedless of
much-burdened clouds, bird cages rock and toss in waves
as tethered and responding to bungee cords
colour-coded 'pigeon', 'jackdaw', 'woodpecker',

      these cages keep obedient birds
on song, the species sing out of their hymnbooks by name,
mellifluous passages smooth what-needs-must-be,
        storms abate,
      on basalt shelves, in courtyards limed with
flocks puffed out in niche groups,
whether switched to Random or to Automatic Cycle,
heads turn in unity, the program dumps

spattering outcrops featureless and rude, infesting domes.
      Reset wing. Squelch. Reset eye.
Jerked forward on conveyors, fledged on set frequency
      insensitive to marsh calls, dead-set –
cut a break by star-effects

glowing on-line, drawing down their stations
through bamboo fretwork or via phone mast volleys/
        reset, reset/ *identify by name* —

Defibrillate! Revive! Kick-name them so they lurch
    splay-winged, nail
them to a tessellated door like articles, or
shuddering like feather-grass or boas. Whereat they dip
    for guidance systems, pass for Truth
    across the tasked clouds
to Morocco, Algiers. Little harbingers crank.
Their elastic cords twitch. Far as they go, swerve in folly

tangled amid cords and discords,
    dialysis directs them in their visible strains
to this or that appointed bourn, that hedge, that thing,
                 and on the thermals they
    separate, their cries heard
by mariners who near the coast, by nomads
nearing habitation. Earth glows in pockets, beckoning,
song filaments float above the labourers pressing forward.

# 6

Just have your footsteps faltering a tactful way off-account.
Any part a set-aside like a meadow drains off pain.
4 hard-boiled eggs rattle in the pan rep Singapore parody
    Liberty, sweet Liberty.
                An orange shell-suit
hangs from its weighed bough.
Conductors with machine-guns among the beads at inter-
sections giggle then stiffing faces,

rotating on their podiums, trained along the shadow edge,
their eyes alert and empty
skin shadow off stone,
    the curve-leg, the straight-leg, the short-leg
stick out to wiggle, majuscules
populate strong light. Loud traffic hushes,
car transporters shrug off cars on the verge, pits
and raw stripes write exercises notarising bone and joint –

Sing it again, Liberty, sweet Liberty, tuned by
    season, beleaguered /it of it of it/
footprints of birds in drying concrete, orange leaves
skittering, motor burn fingers, who
    prepares the Involute, horror
then relief conforming song as to her contraterrene;
so also by its crushed possibilities, its crushed possibilities
smell of fire, she shall force forward fiercely

un-elsed, un-othered: eggs rattle in a snag-tooth brake,
concordant reach true temper even as thrust to her knees
    it of it of it, in each case
    a smattering
    regardless of the nettle window,
it of it of it,
despite the collapsed wheat submissions, barley
at this altitude, even as the card melts her name raised,
in metadata lost between formats she shows up

unsorted. By 5 o'clock plucked-up mist starts to crest,
                    killer
beats diaphragm the walls, they are unremitting.
          Plausible and tanned a gatekeeper
turns a cheek stripped of its shadow, taps out
        versions of invented Instinct,
                        messenger of that
amine for the plucking-up. This inside That that has inside
courses gathering and splaying, matter-woven
            It of it of it —


                    leaves commingle,
rucked under bird-lime and snails slick the earth. Starved
children forage
after peg fungi, scrabble through topsoil,
scale along creepers, down chiffon bark, down soft mace.
                    In the scaffold
throbs hanging fruit not to harvest. Glowing
wait for their format, wait for the
messenger to bring red catechol so as to interrupt:

It is the dead of day. Commotion stills,
        all companions lie as though comatose from self.
This is a Special Purpose Vehicle and the future swoops
to re-attach their tongues. Then they settle down,
        millions not yet living
speak with one voice. The mining companies
truck in dayworkers who look at first like the ideal match,
yet what does a strip search show.


                    It of it of it.

## 7

Here hangs, here constellates. Suspended till earth bursts
over a tumulus/ Emptiness my greeter, pair of shoes
Would you call them hard up, lime splashes
rows of imperial busts. Soft percussion
bats at glass,
pollinators volume the stint strings.
    Here lays off. Here an Event concurs
down gravel paths where privet walls restrict outbursts,

soft bowls of colour swing on chains, taking their turn to
flaunt pimple echo at misspoke perigee.
    Evacuated forms
dangle whilst their skinliness
thins out, rose petals in a bowl lose all semblance of rose,
fingers that visited withdraw, a gentle brown
    creeps from cranks where petals meet, pushes
to the fringe their reminiscences of pink.

So lick the shadow off rock: Would you scrape away dawn,
washing red the dissected lights, minarets or
conventicle of spiders.
A former wheel-clamper now himself detained
    stares at skies revolving.
    A former nightclub bouncer comes to.
A one-time security officer
can handle this, no problems, mineral known as bazirite.

What will protect you from the touch?
Hand in glove to work remotely on an impervious skull.
A landrace cross, a market garden run to seed
    frocks its purple.
Hands tremble round a shaky radial orbit/
    petals moths linger on/
befalling over sweet heads going sere.
Pull the remote hands out of their cross-chirrup antiphon.

So what will slop the bowl of light? —
streaking the morning's ruffle, break into song, sufficient
staying viable between scalps. Time of day is
dragging through articulate
trees in timed sectors, each a block
starlings tumble out of, carved for accord with
fleet fingers, ribboned like the bands over an astrolabe
throwing V-shaped shadows harrowing its skin-deep sense.

Worked one August there, legendary nights,
        then fell off the map.
Of course I managed well, he was coach, he showed me I
was OK. Hearing nothing later I gave up.
        Did the harbinger just up sticks too?
Volumes collapse such as a thumbed wasabi sachet or a
reddening lump marks.
                Sempiternal cup that
sky of sky of sky.
        Nail
sky of sky of sky.                    Scalp fontanelle.

# 8

Pain about the ankle was but meta-
carpal returning to the fold. This other
budding output, what would you be doing?

The best of it was prepared. No matter
how you fall or where you post your valiant
shoreline, the union of patternmakers

stands on its mettle. None of that would
count were it not for you. It must continue,
the objects want their pockets and their

felt linings, but their balkiness brings
the inconceivability of air
swinging free of hinges of the one fastening

battening its joys, imbuing that squall
neither one can reach through for a second.

## 9

Ensphering air will swaddle the defenceless, on one slope
    Cheek press.
Under stems of rain the open vowel field quivers
       rankled Emptiness. Tap its rim.
The face once applied finds out hollows and would
    funnel through Vacancies. Bloody
clouds numbered like days ratchet down from Parnassus
then splurge over a stool.

What is this stuff?     I do not bend to pick up,
       I do not check every pass,
having been stacked neatly and then staged beside a hedge
of longitudinal seedlings,
    a backdrop of wavelets or of harrowed soil.
       This is Nothing more or less
composited with no face,
with no eye to futurity but a set of ploughed cancellations:

neither will its blades be lifted,
    self-bracketing, self-haloing, possibly its light
issued from a star that never wert or if it were, struck out.
How shall zinc analogues level?
     Where shall stakes be driven?
Unless the gatekeeper gives his all-clear abducts inchoate.
Privet blocks the parterre, a grid
bees get bearings by, gloss and matt checkerboard

    puffs its starry sperm smell,
bees home collaborative the while dip-reporting swallows
    paste over ripples
contouring air. I cannot gauge their pitch. Digits
through their pipes and cartilage
siphon thundersqualls. What kind of fuckery
is this, issuing despatch orders, haloing self, that
being-so, dilapidated coup part slew of Parnassian strings

hooped through turbulence, combing air/
swirl of birdsong turbine-chopped/ sphinctering
*That thing That thing That thing:*
     Children lunge for goodies on the organ track
     Clouds edged in rust pink get hung on
pousse, ruled and barometric wind I
have to say I have to say without stint. Birds grip
acoustic wires, shaping up in genera, bunch in subfamilies
       Such was the shit-storm from which I blew

colour-tagged. Mercator net crackles a closed surface:
     Picking up his tag he
   shoots tongue, the straight ridge is cleared,
across his brow
   air shrinks, convulsive as it channels
through an FX box, as reverb
buffets cages skewing songs tuned to Berber villages, Atlas
mountain clefts, readings flash from beam scales:

the Table of the Hand
swipes and plunges at tumbler LEDs,
        down the blue screen they are dripping
disjunct. Imaginary lure. A swaying tree outflanked a ger-
undive Manifest, a ruched skirt.
Flushed and swollen cheek of cloud gloom lets rip,
         miscellaneous birds spray, unfledge
:   A black chandelier pelts down glass.
Nor could I find light within to make a figure out against.

## 10

My breast with tender pity swells. Lungs hanging
off their pegs, a heart dangles. Peewit
punctuates a timely edge as if to assuage earth's gaping.
Global courses hook tight, twist
round the bird's dragline, tensing to full extent.
Seeds strewn at random, pelted on japanned struts,
shake cages bobbing, cordage
strains to bring the Calculable. If courses in time

arrive without terminus, smart fibres bunch to
sort ends chopped for Congruity:
                        swinging low
above small farms, a nucleus infolding rolls and yaws,
asphalt bruised by wires sparking.
            What separation/spread ratio applies?
Avail me should I of such song-
clouds heave as in birth-spasm throwing voice company:

grey dishevelled birds collapse in clouts. A captive wren
falls, sky shatters whirling powder blue smalts,
tongues fitted into slots hinging fluently and laths
            wheel apart.
                    What left this residue
crusting on outcrops while night thins
shuttered though it is, shuttered and balked, stuff
shook along the grading trays, sluiced with weak acid –

car alarms shriek and chatter mockery of crows,
a new rough edge of doves choking off flow at outlets.
            There is a humming overhead.
            Dust shuffles.
Tongues cosset corrugate spur bill-&-coo,
    stop-packed depths
wafting call-&-response through the shades wings stir,
echo in exchange cells, tweeting underfoot stir:

Thought stirring bulges its vesicles, thinking-through
    leaks from sutures, colonies of thought
        cellulate,
veins once perfused clip off.
        Gulls unsupported plunge into negative.
    Spallation products
smash through their ceiling. Fields of spall
      ramp to depose stars, teats blink distress to monitors,
           dust hardens in venous tracts,
blockage swells My breast with tender pity swells: –

hearts click in the banlieues, gather with enraged squalls
about the ring road/
        jostle clouds forced to piss
myself or parch, compel stunned fingers
and ligatures assemble hemistich clamour slats.
Curlews keen round their perimeter,
    a cloud sachet hardly slakes,
spits a mother vinegared in fistfuls bursts then regorges.
A door gives. An aspirator coughs. The gatekeeper

lets a door slam back and forth absently: Seize title
to his flightless strip, his campaign, his long
view claiming the saturated Foreground, centre stage.
    On her turntable a kneeling
detainee sings and
calls up the gases. Liberty, oh Liberty
      chimes the one tempor-
ality, pendant from a leaden plate above her. To be swept
light, diamond trash. The sun's Sway

mediates, repeats, a row of marigolds planted out
in time-lapse, bends east, moths sink into
laboured Coalescence:
    clouds clap thunderous through the biomass.
The signature of each bee and each flower shifts orbit,
cuts its edge. What is called Peewit calls.
    Distance would become an intensifier.
Magnetic bands launch birds in due rankings. Now rotate:

Not having been born sails into its trammels.
Cloth gets thrown over its every cage.

# Green Tara

*Forbearance is supreme ascetic practice*


Δ


So lorries speak in reversing, and only in reversing,
    then with a great sigh stop. Hh.
Nothing goes forward
beyond some consignment chit, nothing
tests the water except indifferent sky
       backlit by a memory of water.
No change in outlook follows:
criss-crossed with webs of theodolites and tapes,
    distributing pressure
evenly on this abstract topography
         neither here nor there spreads,
precedent just gets swallowed, afterword choked
off in mid-.
     Uncollapsed like a dowsing rod,
a pure deictic,
each road and rail extends from its sheath, glints
icy within range. Scent of water,
one gleam expands.
      What more was necessary. Felt wrung out.
Check off and then keep the pink copy.
Clouds alone move.
Reservoirs in reserve for reservoirs.
All the chill cabinet's shelves in decidedly fizzy light
accommodate their dusked sky. Hh.

Δ

      Felt will be used to cover tracks
that they should claim a new birth on their watch.
      Set unblinking on its stanchion
copious eye thrust its share forth brutally,
more than came to light, than ever did, earth-
moving tracks, surveillance our true soil, ever-
focus-prevalent, tightening
and loosening but thin.
      Where are the machines?
          Flat-beds were shunted forward.
          The once-nomadic probe raked
   its salt and mica lines below
declining mountains –
      Where are the machines?
Machines are gasping on flat-bed bogies
    Machines entranced in their thoughts
Held in reserve suited-up in wrap-around disdain,
                  steel glaciers
jolting over grassland
activate sediment for telecast, open-source,
    loosened to loess.

Δ

A flag is disappearing in thin air. Then appears
        thrills its hyperbolic sponsor. High-altitude
policy applies to herders who line up.
             Voltaic pile.
   Take a snap or thread a long
position through the eyes of local squalls, such
     effects scarcely felt through permafrost.
Stillness at this speed pins travellers on board.
Yes to this chilblain plot, settlers gravitate:
              soon get plugged, get fixed.
Sentry gaze rotates on its gantry, don't mistake
thinning air for a sun-strike, Aegean
     shell
spat off its burning belt.
          Neither is this lunar circum-
scription:
fixed and sensible the generator draws breath,
     as designed the generator
separates flapping stripes, undoes waves, the alas-
   jubilant, compelled and impulsive
               into their neat sockets.
        Everyone follows. Axiomatic. Hence
will be crushed, sifted what was so encompassed.

Δ

Blink. I love you. Blink. Broaching
our new treaty. A blink might trade henceforward
rocks for a thought of rocks.
A gleaming rind about its felted patch.
        Cement will be funnelled, concrete poured,
                sand like noonday shadows
flood robust tents and drive animals
drenched from their pounds.
        In the open
shadows make them skittish,
once out there a spotlight burns them and tracks,
driving them beyond normal range.
        What directs these expulsions?
With increasing distance footfalls
jerk the dowsing rod more violently: get?
        Under snowy outlines
a herdsman rides a thin horse on a dilapidated road,
        far scaling from his tent.
An hour away a woman stamps in clogs.
        Below the pastures
barley is steeped. These are old technologies.
        Unlike our raised earth, sending
military vehicles along its vertebrae,
jetting breaths of ammonia up from permafrost
through punctures, through ruts.
        Blink. These are the findings.
        Blink. This is my marrow.
        Blink. This is a skull polyps button.

Δ

          Blink. Submit visa. At a blink, validate
right of passage to expanses humming,
route via one portal,
portal that must validate before lorries pass,
portal that extends to the plain as its equivalent,
                 so much shook
                 so much shaken out.
    Peer down the telescopic, bring one dot
into the square.
All is one, dots merge to fill the unending scroll,
rain aggregates in columns
in a flat building by a paddy by the Pearl River.
    All is one, borders thickly brushed
where diggers bog down and grunt free,
      jerked along spines of data.
                Hush.
We cannot harp on massed things.
                An iron furnace with repoussé
flowers, rough sorts who hug, chug from glasses
of thick salted tea, confidences,
     who steps out now amongst these?
            Blink. That is her droplet.
Blink. I saw her yet she never had been cleared
to pass.
            So many
            thimble-dockets.
Brushed-against contaminants seek to latch on.

Δ

When on its flat-bed the sun pulls away –
    it never will have pulled away –
a smiling couple occupies the bright ellipse of calm
amidst sorting sheds and washhouses.
Their retro hair says much about them.
Their formal hair is telling.
       Wary smiles ripple
talented from their cocoon, air too
infiltrates like watered silk
fleeting accidents across the day, making
light of them for feudal thinkers,
     strip-mining temporal conditions,
crushing showers, fracking meteors and breezes.
Round the lovers soldiers rush to prop parasols,
piano stools, flower vases, tree silhouettes,
     parkland and mind
unbobbin in a scrim off the stock image bolt
wavering and warped.
But then the scrim felts. Or should.
There should be a kind of thickness at high altitude.
There should be a fulfilment to approach.

Δ

Though each disdained for arid sentiment, if
mutterings stick against a light-startled scrim, and
like moths in their thousands such askings
give us substance in facing one another
then to burrow
through air so high and thin exposure
without felt would kill
      Should it be understood
   this is pressed felt:
   this is a thick blue dyed wool:
These are tents we stretch so as to screen out
skirmishes and drone strikes but even while
pentimenti scratch the surfaces, while ridges of
nothing-much deflect,
ghosts beneath feel like our vertebrae
ribbing tents, feel like we were thrown skins:
In hyperbaric chambers
     technicians ready themselves, machines
are dribbling outside. Exposure had thinned us out
even before the glacial plate scraped.

# Δ

Reach is total in theory so I crouch
below the steel security blind to open up promptly,
        a trainee technician, do my best.
Once switched on, the point of origin
amplifies across the lone and level,
such is fabric without depth, who goes there
embodies in the felted wall, so that a poor signal
wears a genealogy, ranks of coats
soaking up the sun as it strengthens in float glass,
        sombre coats
soak up every colour, flags and lintels,
idols in the forecourts, brilliant numbered persons
leant as though a plush woven coop, get trans-
ported where lippy guides want –
        A deep breath:
This is a breath in *extremis*,
    touchscreen response
toxicates rough barley, melts solder
residues, axles the decoupled wheels turning soffit
of the sky such transits ruck, butter smoke
scrawls under. I can advise on mobile devices
        worm into the distances,
taking that much out of us, gold, green, crimson
spilt and zeroing, within purview of my Supervisor.

Δ

Steel combs interlock, lay tracks before glaciers
scrunch to a rawish gape.
                    Hh. Air brakes sigh.
     Loaded skins
             hydraulic jacks budge, settle down.
Shutters have been heard to lap high lakes.
             Restless
scree slides over surfaces, flaps and tumblers
do their figures briskly. Shuffling breezes
flip titles,
         between hills the forum swivels round,
the democratic forum.
Hh the people sigh,
square guttered like a butcher's block,
                    bank
             facing flecked with mica, its anti-climb, its anti-
vandal finish pre-stressed devoid of motion.
                    Comminuted stone
tips into thick grid-force under-mesh, trite
hopes bond
beneath vainglorious flags, the gate guardians
     kneel, their breast displays
track the sell price of promethium.
Wicks by the thousand stink. Butter lamps smoke.
Manufactured parts, components, cash ruts.
         Hh. Breath dissipates.

Δ

      Here Forward is the only gear engaged,
    invisibles
pull their weight, rare earth futures reach
maturity on piton-bristled faces, claw
        capless mountains,
      resistance wisps away in wraps of green mist:
        Human drafts that Logistics rounds up
      get cracking, fall to work:
pails, hods, tippers queue to disgorge
as though nihil obstats from
      remunerative universes
ceaselessly were issued no matter whose cargo or
    where an end-user ended-up
      had the thought to thicken,
churn mire by slag and slurry pits behind a row of
forced settlements:

A single drop of water lets fall a memory of water
as water.
A single drop sears the skin.
Contact at the ear is aflame.
Then you respond without let or contrivance,
    advance the face wanted so to nothing want,
lean in from a dying world.
Reply in round on a self shying gamut.
No reversing without guidance of the banksman.
        Droplet of water. Green stealth.

# Notes and Acknowledgments

*A Claim to Land By the River*
Adrian Adams was a British-American anthropologist who in 1975 set out to study Sininke agricultural systems in the village of Kounghani in Senegal. Four years later she returned to settle there as a wife of Jaabé So, leader of a federation of peasant co-operatives. With him she wrote the classic work of anthropological activism, *A Claim to Land by the River* (Oxford UP 1996). She died in a road accident on her way to Dakar in 2000.

These poems were written between 2004 and 2013.

*Ode at the Gate of the Gathering* appeared as a pamphlet from Crater Press, Brighton, England, at Christmas 2011.

*Courses Matter-Woven* was published as a pamphlet by Equipage, Cambridge, England, in 2015.

'In Suffrance' was posted on-line at Infinite Editions as a web postcard designed by Francis Hunt, in 2013.

'Lyric' was published as a broadside by Squircle Line Press, Singapore, 2014.

Other poems, usually in earlier versions, appeared in the print journals *Chicago Review, Damn the Caesars, halfcircle, Mute, Notre Dame Review, Penumbra, The Poker, This Corner, VerseVersion* (with Chinese translations by Zhao Gu) and *Vlak* and in the web journals *Black Box Manifold, GreatWorks, Green Integer Review, Jacket, Jerry, Salt, Signals Magazine,* and *Spine.*

John Wilkinson is a British poet who has had two distinct careers, in mental health services in the United Kingdom as a nurse, social worker, and policy maker, and subsequently as a university teacher in the United States where he now chairs Creative Writing and Poetics at the University of Chicago. *Ghost Nets* is his tenth book of poetry, and the first to be published in the United States.

Ghost Nets
by John Wilkinson

Cover art by Patrick Chamberlain, "now I lay me down to sleep" (2015),
Collection of Lynn Hauser and Neil Ross

Cover text set in Century Gothic and Johanna MT Std
Interior text set in Century Gothic and Johanna MT Std

Cover and interior design by Sharon Zetter

Offset printed in the United States
by Edwards Brothers Malloy, Ann Arbor, Michigan
On 55# Enviro Natural 100% Recycled 100% PCW
Acid Free Archival Quality FSC Certified Paper

Publication of this book was made possible in part by gifts from:
The New Place Fund
Robin & Curt Caton

Omnidawn Publishing
Oakland, California
2016

Omnidawn Staff & Volunteers
Rusty Morrison & Ken Keegan, senior editors & co-publishers
Gillian Olivia Blythe Hamel, managing editor
Cassandra Smith, poetry editor & book designer
Peter Burghardt, poetry editor
Sharon Zetter, poetry editor, book designer & development officer
Liza Flum, poetry editor & marketing assistant
Juliana Paslay, fiction editor
Gail Aronson, fiction editor
Kevin Peters, marketing assistant & OmniVerse Lit Scene editor
Cameron Stuart, marketing assistant
Sara Burant, administrative assistant
Avren Keating, administrative assistant
Josie Gallup, publicity assistant
SD Sumner, copyeditor